A POIROT DOUBLE BILL

by Agatha Christie

SAMUEL FRENCH

samuelfrench.co.uk

Copyright © 1932, 1937 Agatha Christie Limited. All Rights Reserved.
'AGATHA CHRISTIE', 'POIROT' and the Agatha Christie Signature
Mark and the AC Monogram logo are registered trademarks of Agatha
Christie Limited in the UK and elsewhere. All Rights Reserved.

A POIROT DOUBLE BILL is fully protected under the copyright laws of the British Commonwealth, including Canada, the United States of America, and all other countries of the Copyright Union. All rights, including professional and amateur stage productions, recitation, lecturing, public reading, motion picture, radio broadcasting, television and the rights of translation into foreign languages are strictly reserved.

ISBN 978-0-573-03105-2

concordtheatricals.co.uk
concordtheatricals.com
www.agathachristielimited.com

For Production Enquiries

United Kingdom and World Excluding North America

licensing@concordtheatricals.co.uk
020-7054-7200

United States and Canada

Info@concordtheatricals.com
1-866-979-0447

Each title is subject to availability from Samuel French, depending upon country of performance.

CAUTION: Professional and amateur producers are hereby warned that *A POIROT DOUBLE BILL* is subject to a licensing fee. Publication of this play does not imply availability for performance. Both amateurs and professionals considering a production are strongly advised to apply to the appropriate agent before starting rehearsals, advertising, or booking a theatre. A licensing fee must be paid whether the title is presented for charity or gain and whether or not admission is charged.

No one shall make any changes in this title for the purpose of production. No part of this book may be reproduced, stored in a retrieval system, or transmitted in any form, by any means, now known or yet to be invented, including mechanical, electronic, photocopying, recording, videotaping, or otherwise, without the prior written permission of the publisher. No one shall upload this title, or part of this title, to any social media websites.

For all enquiries regarding motion picture, television, and other media rights, please contact Samuel French.

The right of Agatha Christie to be identified as author of this work has been asserted in accordance with Section 77 of the Copyright, Designs and Patents Act 1988.

MUSIC USE NOTE

Licensees are solely responsible for obtaining formal written permission from copyright owners to use copyrighted music in the performance of this play and are strongly cautioned to do so. If no such permission is obtained by the licensee, then the licensee must use only original music that the licensee owns and controls. Licensees are solely responsible and liable for all music clearances and shall indemnify the copyright owners of the play(s) and their licensing agent, Samuel French, against any costs, expenses, losses and liabilities arising from the use of music by licensees. Please contact the appropriate music licensing authority in your territory for the rights to any incidental music.

IMPORTANT BILLING AND CREDIT REQUIREMENTS

If you have obtained performance rights to this title, please refer to your licensing agreement for important billing and credit requirements.

TABLE OF CONTENTS

The Wasp's Nest 9
Yellow Iris 29

The Wasp's Nest

CHARACTERS

CHARLES HARBOROUGH
CLAUD LANGDON
NINA BELLAMY
HERCULE POIROT

SETTING

The garden of Charles Harborough's house about half an hour before sunset on a summer's evening.

THE WASP'S NEST was originally a television play broadcast on the BBC on 18 June 1937. It was broadcast live from Alexandra Palace as part of the programme Theatre Parade. It was directed by George More O'Ferrall and the cast was as follows:

CHARLES HARBOROUGH . . . . D.A. Clarke-Smith
CLAUD LANGDON . . . . Wallace Douglas
NINA BELLAMY . . . . Antoinette Cellier
HERCULE POIROT . . . . Francis L. Sullivan

(The garden of **CHARLES HARBOROUGH**'s *house. There is a wall with a door leading to the road. Near the door is a tall shrub. There is a table with drinks and garden chairs and an old tree root can be seen which contains a wasp's nest.* **NINA BELLAMY** *and* **CLAUD LANGDON** *are together. She is a pretty girl of twenty. At the moment she looks worried and upset. He is a good looking fellow of twenty-seven. He has a sullen expression on his face and is refusing to look at her.)*

NINA. *(Pleadingly.)* You do see how it was, don't you, Claud?

CLAUD. *(Reluctantly.)* Yes, I see.

NINA. And you forgive me?

 (He does not answer.)

 You do forgive me?

CLAUD. *(Impatiently.)* Oh, of course, of course! We've been over all that.

 (He speaks to himself.)

 But it's a bad show.

NINA. What?

CLAUD. Nothing, my dear.

NINA. You're so queer and unlike yourself.

CLAUD. Well, I feel rather badly about the business that's all.

NINA. It was my fault – all my fault. I blame myself bitterly.

CLAUD. You mustn't do that. It was my fault as much as yours. I was a bad tempered overbearing brute. No wonder you couldn't put up with me.

(**HERCULE POIROT** *enters. He stands in the doorway unnoticed, observing the two young people.*)

NINA. Yes, but I needn't have –

CLAUD. *(Impatiently.)* Oh, don't let's go over it all again.

NINA. I want you to understand.

CLAUD. I do understand.

NINA. And you do forgive me?

(**CLAUD** *takes* **NINA** *in his arms and kisses her gently.*)

And now you really have forgiven me?

CLAUD. For the thousandth time, yes!

NINA. *(Recoiling.)* But you are still angry, though.

CLAUD. Let's wash the subject out once and for all. Are you coming?

NINA. Not now. I'm waiting to see Charles.

CLAUD. *(Rudely.)* And more talk – talk – talk! Sorry, Nina, I'm in a bad mood today.

(*He turns sharply to exit and collides with* **POIROT**.)

POIROT. Pardon!

CLAUD. Sorry. My fault.

POIROT. Not at all, Mr. Langdon.

CLAUD. *(Surprised.)* You know me?

POIROT. I saw your name, *(Pause.)* at the chemist's shop.

(**CLAUD** *looks a little disconcerted.*)

CLAUD. Oh! The chemist's shop…

POIROT. Precisely. The chemist's shop.

CLAUD. *(Uncertainly.)* Oh!

(*He exits brusquely.* **POIROT** *bows politely to* **NINA**.)

POIROT. Mademoiselle!

> *(He looks slowly round as though in search of something.)*

NINA. *(Coldly.)* Do you – er – want anything?

POIROT. It is true that I search for something.

NINA. What?

POIROT. A wasp's nest.

> *(**NINA** looks at him as if he is mad.)*

NINA. These are private grounds, you know.

POIROT. *(Searching.)* Mais oui, mais oui.

NINA. So unless you wish to see Mr. Harborough –

POIROT. *(Absently.)* Monsieur Harborough, yes.

NINA. *(Sharply.)* This is Mr. Harborough's estate.

POIROT. I know. It is to see my friend Monsieur Harborough that I come.

NINA. *(Relieved.)* Oh, I see!

POIROT. *(Cheekily.)* So you see, Mademoiselle, I am not quite so mad as you think.

NINA. Oh, I didn't –

POIROT. But you did. You showed it most plainly. Now however, you are reassured. I am the friend of the family. My character is cleared.

NINA. I did think that perhaps –

> *(She breaks off and laughs.)*

I suppose I showed it rather plainly.

POIROT. I am very quick to see things.

> *(He looks at her attentively.)*

I can see something else. That you are worried, Mademoiselle.

NINA. Oh!

> *(She turns abruptly away. **CHARLES HARBOROUGH**, a man of about forty, enters.)*

CHARLES. *(Surprised.)* Nina!

NINA. *(Nervously.)* Yes, I – I wanted to see you.

(**CHARLES** *catches sight of* **POIROT**.)

CHARLES. By all that's wonderful, Hercule Poirot!

(*He shakes him warmly by the hand.*)

NINA. (*Startled.*) Hercule Poirot!

CHARLES. Monsieur Poirot – Miss Bellamy. The prince of detectives, Nina. The terror of evil-doers.

(*He turns back to* **POIROT**.)

And what brings you to this quiet part of the world?

POIROT. You remember saying to me if ever I am in this part of the country to look you up. That is right, is it not? Look you up!

CHARLES. Quite right.

POIROT. Eh bien, I take you at your word.

CHARLES. Splendid. Have a drink.

NINA. I – I think I'll be going Charles. I'll see you tomorrow.

(*She slips out quickly.*)

POIROT. No whisky – a little plain soda only. That was your fiancée, was it not? All the congratulations.

CHARLES. Oh – er – you saw?

POIROT. But yes, I read the announcement three days ago. A marriage arranged between Charles Harborough and Nina, the daughter of Colonel Bellamy.

(*He raises his glass.*)

À votre santé.

(**CHARLES** *turns away sharply with a gesture that might be embarrassment or dislike.*)

You are a fortunate man.

CHARLES. (*Gruffly.*) Yes.

(*They sit.*)

POIROT. The young lady is charming – quite charming.

(*There is a pause.*)

Pardon me if I commit an indiscretion – the lady was engaged before she met you?

CHARLES. Yes.

POIROT. To a Mr. Langdon?

CHARLES. Yes.

POIROT. So she has done the jilt, as you say. She has turned him downwards for you?

CHARLES. Yes, but –

POIROT. Which is all very well for you, but not so agreeable for him, eh?

CHARLES. *(Stiffly.)* It's a lady's privilege to change her mind, and if you'll excuse my saying so, Monsieur Poirot, jilting is rather an offensive expression.

POIROT. *(Quickly.)* Ah! Pardon.

CHARLES. *(Sententiously.)* It's better to find out a mistake in time.

POIROT. Much better. And Mr. Langdon, what does he think?

CHARLES. Langdon's taken it very well, taken it like a man, in fact.

POIROT. Like a man. How does a man take a thing of that kind?

CHARLES. Like a sportsman.

POIROT. *(Thoughtfully.)* Ah!

CHARLES. You've not told me what you are doing down in this part of the world. On holiday, I suppose?

POIROT. *(Slowly.)* No, I am not on holiday. I am here on business.

CHARLES. Business?

(He stares curiously at **POIROT.***)*

You mean you are here professionally – as a detective?

POIROT. Yes.

CHARLES. *(Curiously.)* I suppose I mustn't ask you anything about your investigations?

POIROT. On the contrary, I should prefer that you asked.

CHARLES. You are investigating a – burglary?

POIROT. Something far more serious.

CHARLES. What?

POIROT. *(Quietly.)* Murder.

CHARLES. *(Startled.)* You mean –

POIROT. *(Impressively.)* Murder!

CHARLES. But I haven't heard of any murder.

POIROT. No, you would not have heard of it.

CHARLES. Who has been murdered?

POIROT. As yet, nobody.

CHARLES. Oh!

>*(He leans back with a laugh.* **POIROT** *remains serious.)*

POIROT. That is why I said you would not have heard of it. Nobody has been murdered yet. I am investigating a crime that has not yet taken place.

CHARLES. But look here, that's nonsense!

POIROT. Not at all. If one can investigate a crime before it has happened, surely that is very much better than investigating it afterwards. You see, one might prevent it.

CHARLES. You're not serious, Monsieur Poirot?

POIROT. But yes, I am serious.

>*(**CHARLES** is impressed in spite of himself.)*

CHARLES. You really believe that a murder is going to be committed?

POIROT. I know it.

CHARLES. You are making me feel quite eerie.

>*(He shivers.)*

Someone must be walking over my grave.

>*(There is a short pause then* **POIROT** *leans forward with a change of manner.)*

POIROT. Tell me, Mr. Harborough, have you a wasp's nest in this garden?

>(**CHARLES** *stares at him.*)

CHARLES. Rather odd your saying that.

POIROT. No, it is not odd, really.

CHARLES. *(Continuing.)* But as a matter of fact there is a nest over there.

>(*He nods towards the tree root.*)

I'm expecting Langdon any minute to take it for me. He's rather good at that sort of thing. Just taken four in his own garden. My gardener's a fool at the job. I said so and Langdon insisted on coming over this evening and doing it.

POIROT. What method does he employ?

CHARLES. Squirts petrol down with a syringe.

POIROT. There is another method. Cyanide of potassium.

CHARLES. Yes, but that's dangerous stuff.

POIROT. Deadly poison.

CHARLES. It's not the kind of stuff I care to have about the place.

POIROT. And yet – just now, Mr. Langdon was buying cyanide of potassium at the chemist.

CHARLES. *(Shocked.)* What?

POIROT. That surprises you?

CHARLES. Yes, it does. What did he say he wanted it for?

POIROT. To take a wasp's nest in your garden, I understood.

CHARLES. Nonsense! He knows I won't have that stuff used. He agreed himself that petrol is much safer and just as efficacious.

POIROT. Then it was not you who asked him to get cyanide?

CHARLES. *(Emphatically.)* Certainly not.

>(**POIROT** *relaxes and sits back.*)

POIROT. That is odd.

CHARLES. It's very odd, very odd indeed.

>(*He looks unhappily at* **POIROT** *who returns his glance steadily. A feeling of tension grows.*)

CHARLES. You're not – not suggesting – no, that's impossible.
POIROT. What is impossible?
CHARLES. That Langdon is – oh! But that's fantastic.
POIROT. Is it?

> *(He gives **CHARLES** a very significant glance.)*

CHARLES. So that's why you came down here, to warn me against Langdon.

> *(He springs up.)*

Oh, but it's absurd.
POIROT. Listen. When I came here this evening, Miss Bellamy and Langdon were here in the garden. They did not observe me. She was talking to him, asking him to forgive her, begging him to tell her that he "understood."
CHARLES. How like a woman.
POIROT. Yes.
CHARLES. Well?
POIROT. So that is all you have to say! Well? And suppose it is not well.
CHARLES. I don't know what you're driving at.
POIROT. I will be more clear. Suppose that Mr. Langdon does not find it well at all. That he neither forgives nor understands, that he is planning revenge.
CHARLES. No, no, that's ridiculously melodramatic. Langdon's said to have the devil of a temper, but he would never. Why, he's carried on absolutely as usual. He's been amazingly decent over the whole business. In fact, he's gone out of his way to be extra friendly with me since – since it happened.
POIROT. Amazingly decent. You use the word amazingly – but you are not amazed. Now me, I find his behaviour very odd.
CHARLES. Yes, but you, excuse me, are a foreigner.
POIROT. I knew you would say that! Nobody who is not of the Latin races can feel jealousy – c'est entendu! But

your police courts give that statement the lie. Come, I will put a case to you. Here is a young man badly hit because he has been turned downwards – you see how idiomatic I am! Eh bien, he sets the teeth, he stiffens the knees, he conceals the emotions and he determines to behave exactly as usual – even more so. He will show the world that he is not hard hit at all – au contraire! Life is very amusing! You are engaged today, you are jilted tomorrow, and what of it all?

CHARLES. That's exactly what I have been saying.

POIROT. But supposing that is all the pose – the gigantic bluff. *(Slowly.)* Jealousy...hate...revenge.

CHARLES. That sort of thing simply doesn't happen in England.

POIROT. The English are sometimes incredibly stupid. They think they can deceive anyone, but that no one can deceive them. The sportsman, the good fellow, never will they believe evil of him. And because they are brave but stupid, *(Significantly.)* sometimes they die.

(**CHARLES** *speaks without conviction.*)

CHARLES. I don't believe Langdon would hurt a fly.

POIROT. The lives of flies are not my concern, and though you say that Mr. Langdon is so tender of them, yet you forget that he is even now preparing to take the life of several hundred wasps!

(**CHARLES** *stands irresolute, looking at him.* **POIROT** *springs up and approaches him. He takes* **CHARLES** *by the shoulders and shakes him.*)

Rouse yourself, my friend, rouse yourself! And look where I am pointing.

(He points towards the tree root.)

There, on the bank, by that old root. See you the wasps returning home, placid at the end of the day? In a little hour comes destruction and they know it not. There is no one to tell them. They have not, it seems, a Hercule

Poirot. I told you, Mr. Harborough, that I came here on business. Murder is my business. It is my business before it has happened as well as afterwards. I am here to prevent this murder – and I shall prevent it!

(There is a pause. **POIROT** *calms himself.)*

What time is Langdon coming to do this business of the wasp's nest?

*(***CHARLES** *is convinced but automatically protests.)*

CHARLES. Langdon would never –

POIROT. At what time?

CHARLES. At ten o'clock.

*(***POIROT** *consults his watch.)*

POIROT. And it is now half past nine, good.

CHARLES. But I tell you Langdon would never –

POIROT. Ah, mon dieu! Langdon would never, Langdon would never! Have it your own way. Langdon would never! C'est entendu!

(He readies himself to leave.)

All the same, I return here at ten o'clock.

CHARLES. But really –

POIROT. Langdon would never! C'est entendu. I return only to amuse myself by seeing one of your English sports – the taking of the wasp's nest. I do not stay to argue with you now, because I should only enrage myself. Au revoir till ten o'clock.

(He bows and makes to exit. **CHARLES** *shrugs his shoulders and turns away. He picks up a glass from the table.* **POIROT** *opens the door but as he is about to go, he draws quickly back, shutting the door behind him and hiding behind the shrub.* **CLAUD** *enters carrying a small glass syringe.)*

CHARLES. *(Turning.)* Hullo, you're late.

CLAUD. Just on time, I think. But it's still rather light. We'd better give the last stragglers time to return home. You've got the stuff all right?

CHARLES. Yes, I've got the stuff. Have a drink?

CLAUD. Thanks.

>   (**CHARLES** *pours a whisky and soda and gives it to him. He then pours one for himself.* **CLAUD** *lays down the syringe on the table.*)

(Sitting.) Nina tells me that the famous Monsieur Poirot is down here.

CHARLES. Yes. He came to look me up.

CLAUD. What's he doing down here?

CHARLES. Possibly his job.

CLAUD. You mean detecting?

CHARLES. Possibly.

CLAUD. But, I say, there isn't anything to detect, is there?

>   *(There is a pause.)*

Is there?

CHARLES. Perhaps Monsieur Poirot knows better. *(Grimly.)* Perhaps, by this time tomorrow there may be something to detect.

CLAUD. So there may. Well, cheerio.

>   *(He raises his glass.)*

CHARLES. Cheerio.

>   (**CLAUD** *drinks then sets down his empty glass.* **CHARLES** *only puts his glass to his lips. There is a pause.*)

I wonder, Langdon, if you'd mind coming back tomorrow and taking the nest then – well, tonight I'd rather give it a miss.

CLAUD. Certainly if you like.

>   *(He becomes suddenly incoherent.)*

I'm sorry if – did Nina – or –

CHARLES. *(Harshly.)* Let's leave all that.

CLAUD. Right. Tomorrow then.

CHARLES. Yes, tomorrow. Goodbye, Langdon.

CLAUD. Goodnight.

CHARLES. Goodbye.

>(**CLAUD** *exits. Left alone,* **CHARLES**' *expression slowly changes. He laughs silently. His face becomes the face of the devil. He looks not quite sane. After his mirth is over he takes a small wide-mouthed bottle from his pocket. It has a few crystals in it, which he shakes into his whisky and soda.*)

>(*Then with a handkerchief he carefully wipes fingerprints from the bottle and throws it into the garden.* **POIROT** *emerges from behind the shrub, coming up noiselessly behind him.* **CHARLES** *picks up his glass and puts it to his lips. Before he drinks,* **POIROT** *deftly seizes it from him.*)

(*Turning.*) What –

>(**POIROT** *steps out of* **CHARLES**' *reach.*)

POIROT. I think I had better drink this.

>(*He raises the glass to his lips.* **CHARLES** *screams in frenzy.*)

CHARLES. Don't drink it! For God's sake don't drink it! It's poisoned, I tell you, poisoned!

>(**POIROT** *with a smile drinks.* **CHARLES** *stands appalled shaking all over.* **POIROT** *makes a grimace, wipes his lips with his handkerchief and replaces the glass on the table.*)

My God, cyanide of potassium.

POIROT. No, my friend, you are in error. You see, just now, I made a little exchange.

>(*He takes a bottle from his pocket.*)

This is the cyanide you asked Claud Langdon to get for you. In your pocket I placed a similar bottle containing washing soda. It was quite simple – a clever pickpocket taught me the trick. I excited myself, I take you by the shoulders – so – and sapristi, the change is made.

CHARLES. *(Broken.)* How did you know?

POIROT. I guessed, my friend. I guessed right, that is all.

CHARLES. But how did you guess?

POIROT. I must begin that story yesterday when I saw you come out of a certain doctor's door in Harley Street. I know that doctor, I know for what one consults him, and I saw your face. It was the face of a doomed man.

CHARLES. Doomed – doomed – he gave me two months to live.

POIROT. I was close by you, but you did not see me. You were too preoccupied. And suddenly I saw your expression change. I saw in your eyes that of which I spoke to you this evening – hate – jealousy – the desire for revenge. You did not trouble to conceal them, you thought there was no need. And then you grinned – a devilish exultant grin it was, and I knew something. I knew that I was looking at a murderer. Do not ask me how I knew, just let me assure you that Hercule Poirot could not be mistaken on that point. I was looking at a murderer, but as yet a murderer only in intention. As I tell you, murder is my business. I came down here today to look into the matter.

CHARLES. Go on.

POIROT. I have seen the announcement of your engagement in the paper. The first thing I hear down here is the story of Miss Bellamy's prior attachment to Claud Langdon. Then I happen to go into the chemist and this same Langdon is there buying cyanide of potassium. So it looks, does it not, as though my ideas were all wrong – as though if murder were being planned, it is Claud Langdon who should be planning to murder you. He has the motive and he has the means. So I come up here to see what is the truth of the wasp's nest story, and I see the two young people and I realise without a doubt that it is Langdon whom she loves.

She has quarrelled with him and got engaged to you in a fit of pique, but now she is asking him to forgive and take her back and trying to make him understand how it all came about. So, after all, it is you who have a motive for murder. It is he who has taken the girl from you. And then I lay a few little traps. I speak of the cyanide, and you deny having asked him to get it for you, but I see your eyelids flicker and I know that you are lying. I pretend to have suspicions and very cleverly you increase them. I am to be your star witness against Langdon.

CHARLES. Do you suggest that I meant to poison Langdon with cyanide?

POIROT. No, your crime was cleverer than that! The cyanide was for yourself – a quick death instead of the lingering one the specialist had foretold for you. Langdon was to be accused of your murder. Miss Bellamy's engagement to you would give the motive. Then there would be the purchase of the poison. He would say that he had done that at your request, but then I should give evidence that that was not so, that you had expressly denied having done any such thing. So motive, means and finally – opportunity. He comes up and has a drink with you this evening – and you are found dead with the remains of cyanide in your glass. And so Claud Langdon would have been hanged and Miss Bellamy's heart would have been broken.

(**CHARLES**' *voice is thick with passion.*)

CHARLES. And why not? Why not? Why should he have everything and I nothing? Why should he live and I die? Why should he have Nina? Nina! Nina, who made a fool of me. I hated them both. I wanted them to suffer – suffer – as I suffer! *(Angrily.)* And you – you –

POIROT. I have saved you. Oh, not from death. Death comes to all of us sooner or later. But I have saved you from sending an innocent man to his death, and from ruining a girl's life. Even now in your heart, you are glad that I came here today. *(Compellingly.)* Tell me, my friend, are you not glad that you will die an honest man and not a murderer, thanks to Hercule Poirot.

CHARLES. I – I –

> *(He breaks down. **NINA** and **CLAUD** enter. It has grown almost dark.)*

NINA. Is that you, Charles? We came – I felt we must come tonight –

CLAUD. *(Interrupting.)* Look here, Harborough, the truth of the matter is –

CHARLES. *(Brusquely.)* I know the truth. Nina cares for you, Langdon, and always has. Well, that's all right. No bones broken. Do you mind if I leave you with Monsieur Poirot? He's rather pleased with himself just now. And perhaps he's right.

> *(He puts a hand on **NINA**'s shoulder.)*

Bless you, my dear, be happy.

> *(He exits. **NINA** turns to **POIROT**.)*

NINA. Why are you pleased with yourself?

POIROT. I have succeeded in the business that brought me down here.

NINA. *(Doubtfully.)* Oh?

POIROT. *(Happily.)* And now, a little relaxation. For a change I experience the reactions of murder – murder on a grand scale, you comprehend.

> *(He fills the cyanide bottle with water, shakes it, then tip-toes to the wasp's nest with exaggerated caution. Averting his head, he pours it down a hole in the root. He contemplates the results.)*

POIROT. Voilà. They die the death. Alas, poor wasps, there is none to save you.

> *(He turns to the others.)*

You see, they had no Hercule Poirot!

End of Play

Yellow Iris

CHARACTERS

HERCULE POIROT
PAULINE WEATHERBY
SEÑORA LOLA VALDEZ
BARTON RUSSELL
ANTHONY CHAPPELL
STEPHEN CARTER
WAITER
CLOAKROOM ATTENDANT
COMPÉRE

YELLOW IRIS was first performed on the BBC National Programme on 2 November 1937. The original broadcast was featured with music composed by Michael Sayer and lyrics by Christopher Hassall. The cast was as follows:

HERCULE POIROT . . . . Anthony Holles
PAULINE WEATHERBY . . . . Evelyn Neilson
SEÑORA LOLA VALDEZ . . . . Martita Hunt
BARTON RUSSELL . . . . Sydney Keith
ANTHONY CHAPPELL . . . . Frank Drew
STEPHEN CARTER . . . . Peter Scott
WAITER . . . . Dino Galvani
CLOAKROOM ATTENDANT . . . . Audrey Cameron
COMPÉRE . . . . Bernard Jukes

Scene One

(The restaurant of the hotel Jardin des Cygnes. Mixed restaurant chatter is heard.)

PAULINE. *(Urgently.)* Waiter! Waiter!

WAITER. Mademoiselle?

PAULINE. Where can I telephone? It's desperately urgent.

WAITER. The telephone, mam'selle, is in there.

PAULINE. Thank you.

(The restaurant chatter fades.)

Scene Two

(The hotel lobby. The porter's bell from the front desk is heard. The **CLOAKROOM ATTENDANT** *speaks efficiently as* **SEÑORA LOLA VALDEZ** *arrives.)*

ATTENDANT. Good evening, madam. Can I take your cloak?

LOLA. Yes, please.

ATTENDANT. Thank you, madam.

LOLA. Tell me, the telephone – where is it?

ATTENDANT. The telephone, madam? Just outside this cloakroom, on your right, madam.

LOLA. Ah yes. Thank you. *(Quietly.)* Is it private? I have a very important personal message to give. I would not like anyone to –

ATTENDANT. Quite private, madam. On your right as you go out.

LOLA. Oh, thank you.

(Fade.)

Scene Three

(The study of **HERCULE POIROT**. *The telephone rings.)*

POIROT. Hélas! Never is there peace.

(He calls.)

Jules! Jules! Le téléphone!

(There is no reply. The telephone continues to ring.)

Zut alors!

(He lifts the receiver.)

Hallo!

*(***PAULINE*** speaks, disguising her voice.)*

PAULINE. *(Urgently.)* Is that Monsieur Hercule Poirot? Is that Hercule Poirot?

POIROT. Hercule Poirot speaks!

PAULINE. Monsieur Poirot, can you come at once – at once? I'm in great danger, I know it!

POIROT. Who are you? From where are you speaking?

*(***PAULINE*** sounds more distant.)*

PAULINE. At once… It may be life or death! The Jardin des Cygnes…at once…table with yellow irises –

(The line goes dead.)

POIROT. Hallo! Hallo!

(He rattles the receiver.)

Hallo! *(Quietly.)* The Jardin des Cygnes, hein? There is something here very curious.

(Fade.)

Scene Four

(Restaurant at Jardin des Cygnes. Mixed restaurant chatter and music.)

["YOU'RE GOOD FOR MY BAD HABITS"]

CHORUS
    YOU'RE GOOD FOR MY BAD HABITS,
    I CAN'T REMEMBER NOW
    THE WAY TO SAY, "OH! BLIMEY!"
    TRY ME – NO KIDDIN' –
    YOU'RE GOOD FOR MY BAD HABITS,
    YOU'VE DONE THE TRICK SOMEHOW,
    AND ALL WITHOUT A SINGLE ROW.
    FOR YEARS I'VE WAITED
    FOR SOMEONE THAT LOVED ME YET HATED
    ME BITING MY NAILS.
    YOU GAVE ME SOMETHING TO CARE FOR,
    AND THEREFORE
    I WENT BACK ON THE RAILS.
    YOU'RE GOOD FOR MY BAD HABITS,
    IF I COULD MARRY YOU,
    YOU'D FIND THAT I COULD DO GOOD TOO.

VERSE
    SOME PEOPLE LIVE IN A CHRONIC HURRY,
    NOTHING BUT WORRY
    ALL THE DAY THROUGH
    BUT LIFE WILL MOVE IN A NEW DIRECTION
    WHEN THERE'S AFFECTION
    TO GUIDE YOU.

*(The **CHORUS** reprises over the following dialogue.)*

WAITER. Buona sera, Monsieur Poirot. Welcome to the Jardin des Cygnes. You desire a table, yes?

POIROT. No, no, my good Luigi. I seek here for some friends – perhaps they are not here yet.

WAITER. It is a big party?

POIROT. Non – non. Ah, let me see, that table in the corner with the yellow irises!

WAITER. Yes?

POIROT. A little question, if it is not indiscreet. On all the other tables there are tulips – pink tulips. Why on that one table have you yellow irises?

WAITER. A command, monsieur – a special order. No doubt to please one of the ladies.

POIROT. But of course. And the table is…?

WAITER. Mr. Barton Russell's table – an American. Rich, oh là là, so rich!

POIROT. Aha, and one must study the whims of the ladies, must one not, my good Luigi?

WAITER. Monsieur has said it.

> *(Light applause is heard at the end of the number.)*

POIROT. But tiens, I see at the table an acquaintance of mine. I must go and speak to him!

> *(There is a pause.)*

Bon soir! Bon soir! Is it not my friend Anthony Chappell?

CHAPPELL. By all that's wonderful, Poirot, the police hound. Come and sit down. Let us discourse of crime. Let us go further and drink to crime!

POIROT. Thank you, mon cher Anthony.

> *(An instrumental version of* **YOU LIVE IN MY HEART** *underscores the restaurant chatter.)*

CHAPPELL. There's a glass there!

POIROT. A little only…

CHAPPELL. Now tell me what you're doing here. There isn't a dead body in the place – positively not a single one!

POIROT. You seem very gay, mon cher?

CHAPPELL. Gay? I'm steeped in misery, wallowing in gloom. *(Confidentially.)* You hear this tune they're playing?

POIROT. Yes?

CHAPPELL. You recognise it?

POIROT. Something perhaps to do with your baby having left you?

CHAPPELL. Not a bad guess, but wrong for once. "You Live In My Heart" – that's what it's called!

POIROT. Aha!

CHAPPELL. *(Mournfully.)* My favourite tune – my favourite restaurant and my favourite band. And my favourite girl is here and she's dancing it with someone else!

POIROT. Hence the melancholy?

CHAPPELL. Exactly. Pauline and I, you see, have had what the vulgar call "words." That's to say, she's had ninety-five out of every one hundred. My five are, "But darling, I can explain!" Then she starts in again with her ninety-five and we get no further. I think I shall poison myself!

POIROT. Pauline?

CHAPPELL. Pauline Weatherby. Barton Russell's sister-in-law. Young, lovely, disgustingly rich. This is Barton's party. D'you know him?

POIROT. Non, I have still the pleasure. Who else is at this party?

CHAPPELL. You'll meet 'em in a minute. Forgive me, Monsieur Poirot, but that girl's going to sing.

POIROT. And this being your favourite tune – perhaps the lyric has a special message?

CHAPPELL. Perhaps!

["YOU LIVE IN MY HEART"]

I HAD NO CHOICE BUT TO ADORE YOU
SOON AS I SAW YOU.
UNDER THE MOON
THIS NEW ROMANCE
HAS ONLY JUST STARTED,
WHY MUST WE BE PARTED
SO SOON?
YOU LIVE IN MY HEART,

AND YOU'RE A PART OF ALL THE LOVELINESS
I SEE.
YOU LIVE IN MY DREAMS,
EVEN THE SCHEMES
I MAKE ARE FASHIONED FOR YOU ONLY.
YOU LIVE IN MY HEART,
NO MATTER HOW THE WAVES OF OCEAN ROLL BETWEEN.
RIGHT – RIGHT FROM THE START,
I'VE ALWAYS HELD YOU CLOSE FOR YOU TO LIVE
IN MY HEART.

(Warm applause and mixed chatter is heard.)

(Sighing.) Ah, well!

POIROT. A very "affecting" lyric, mon vieux – but before it, you were telling me who was at this party apart from the charming Miss Weatherby.

CHAPPELL. Oh yes, of course. Well, there's Lola Valdez – you know, the South American dancer in the metropole show. Stephen Carter, he's in the diplomatic – very hush, hush – known as Silent Stephen – he's… Hullo, here they come. Here's somebody I want you to meet –

(There is a pause.)

Barton Russell – Monsieur Hercule Poirot.

RUSSELL. What, is this the great Monsieur Poirot? I'm very glad to meet you, sir. Let me introduce Señora Valdez.

VALDEZ. How do you do?

POIROT. Enchanté, mademoiselle!

RUSSELL. And Miss Weatherby.

POIROT. Enchanté, mademoiselle!

CARTER. How do you do!

RUSSELL. Won't you sit down and join us? That is unless…

CHAPPELL. He's got an appointment with a body, I believe. Or is it an absconding financier?

POIROT. Ah, my friend, do you think I am never off duty? May I not for once seek only to amuse myself?

CHAPPELL. Perhaps you've got an appointment with Carter here? The latest from Geneva! Stolen plans must be found or war declared tomorrow!

PAULINE. *(Cuttingly.)* Must you be so completely idiotic, Tony?

CHAPPELL. Sorry, Pauline.

POIROT. How severe you are, mademoiselle!

PAULINE. I hate people who play the fool all the time.

POIROT. Ah, then I must converse only of serious matters!

PAULINE. Oh no, Monsieur Poirot, I didn't mean you!

POIROT. Ah, bon.

PAULINE. Are you really a kind of Sherlock Holmes and do wonderful deductions?

POIROT. Ah, the deductions – they are not so easy in real life. But shall I try?

PAULINE. Yes, do!

POIROT. Now then, I deduce – that yellow irises are your favourite flowers?

PAULINE. Quite wrong, Monsieur Poirot. Lily of the Valley or roses!

POIROT. *(Sighs.)* A failure. Never mind, I will try once more. This evening, not very long ago, you telehphoned to someone.

PAULINE. Quite right!

POIROT. It was not long after you arrived here?

PAULINE. Right again. I telephoned the minute I got inside doors.

POIROT. Ah, that is not so good. You telephoned *before* you came to this table?

PAULINE. Yes.

POIROT. Decidedly very bad.

PAULINE. Oh no, I think it was very clever of you. How did you know I had telephoned?

POIROT. That, mademoiselle, is a great detective's secret. And the person to whom you telephoned – does his name begin with a P – or perhaps with an H?

PAULINE. *(Laughs.)* Quite wrong. I telephoned to my maid to post some frightfully important letters that I'd never sent off. Her name's Louise.

(Instrumental of "Your Heart Was In My Hands" begins to play.)

POIROT. I am confused – quite confused. Can it be that I need practice? Ah, what charming music. La Valse. Do you not dance, mam'selle?

CHAPPELL. Yes, what about it, Pauline?

PAULINE. I don't think I want to dance again so soon, Tony.

CHAPPELL. Isn't that too bad?

POIROT. Señora Valdez, I would not dare to ask you to dance with me. I am too much of the antique.

VALDEZ. Ah, it is nonsense that you talk there! You are still young. Your hair, it is still black!

(Polite laughter is heard from the group.)

RUSSELL. Pauline, as your brother-in-law, I'm just going to force you on to the floor! This one's a waltz and a waltz is about the only dance I really can do.

PAULINE. Why, of course, Barton. We'll take the floor right away.

RUSSELL. Good girl Pauline, that's swell of you.

PAULINE. Come along then, I'm waiting.

(The restaurant chatter fades as the vocal begins.)

["YOUR HEART WAS IN MY HANDS"]

CAN'T WE RECAPTURE
THE RAPTURE
THAT MADE ALL THE WORLD SEEM GAY?
SURELY TOMORROW
OUR SORROW
WILL FADE ALL AWAY – DWINDLE AWAY.

YOUR HEART WAS IN MY HANDS,
AND YET I LET YOU GO.
WHAT HAVE WE TO SHOW
FOR ALL THE LOVE WE CHERISHED?
YOUR HEART WAS IN MY HANDS
BUT I WAS IN A DREAM,
LIFE APPEARED TO FLOW
JUST LIKE A STREAM.
I KNEW NOT A SAD MORNING
WAS SOON GOING TO BREAK
AND WHEN I WAS AWAKE
REVEAL MY MISTAKE.
YOUR HEART WAS IN MY HANDS
AND MINE HAS VANISHED TOO
MINE SHALL EVER STAY WITH YOU.

> *(An orchestral reprise begins. Mixed chatter is heard.)*

CHAPPELL. Pretty creature Pauline is – especially when she's dancing, eh Carter?

> *(There is a pause.)*

I say, talkative little fellow, aren't you, Carter? Help to make a party go with your merry chatter, eh what?

CARTER. Really, Chappell, I don't know what you mean.

CHAPPELL. Oh, you don't – don't you?

CARTER. My dear fellow.

CHAPPELL. Well, drink man, drink, if you won't talk!

CARTER. No thanks.

CHAPPELL. Then I will.

CARTER. *(Coldly.)* Excuse me, must just speak to a fellow I know over there. Fellow I was at school with.

> *(There is a pause.* **CHAPPELL** *speaks almost to himself.)*

CHAPPELL. Somebody ought to have drowned him at birth.

POIROT. It is not my affair, but were you not a little harsh, mon vieux!

VALDEZ. Poor Mister Carter looks very hurt!

CHAPPELL. Oh, Silent Stephen can look after himself. Does him good.

POIROT. I wonder, may I ask, what are the favourite flowers of mademoiselle?

VALDEZ. *(Archly.)* Ah now, why is it you want to know?

POIROT. Mademoiselle, if I send flowers to a lady, I am particular that they should be flowers she likes.

VALDEZ. That is very charming of you, Monsieur Poirot. I will tell you, I adore the big dark red carnations or the dark red roses.

POIROT. Superb – yes, superb! You do not, then, like yellow flowers – yellow irises?

VALDEZ. Yellow flowers? No, they do not accord with my temperament.

POIROT. How wise. Tell me, mademoiselle, did you ring up a friend tonight, since you arrived here?

VALDEZ. I? Ring up a friend? No, what a curious question.

POIROT. Ah, but I, I am a very curious man.

(Light applause is heard as the number ends.)

VALDEZ. I'm sure you are. And a very dangerous man.

POIROT. No, no, not dangerous – say, a man who may be *useful* in danger!

VALDEZ. *(Giggles.)* No, no. You are dangerous.

POIROT. *(Sighs.)* I see that you do not understand. All this is very strange.

(Instrumental of "Tango Band" begins.)

CHAPPELL. Lola, what about a spot of swoop and dip? Come along.

VALDEZ. I will come, yes. Since Monsieur Poirot is not brave enough!

CHAPPELL. He has no time for frivolous things like dancing. You can meditate on the crime to be committed, old boy!

POIROT. It is profound what you say there. Yes, it is profound...

(The restaurant chatter fades as the vocal begins.)

["THERE'S DANGER IN THE TANGO BAND"]

I KNOW A LADY SO EXOTIC,
SHE'D MAKE A DUMMY FEEL EROTIC,
SHE'S JUST ABOUT AS 'LURING AS CAN BE!
YOU'LL SOON BE SO ENTHUSIASTIC
AND IN THE MOOD FOR SOMETHING DRASTIC,
JUST LISTEN TO ME, WAIT TILL YOU SEE.

THERE'S A WOMAN IN THE TANGO BAND,
SHE'S THE TERROR OF THE TANGO BAND!
LOOK AT THE RINGS TOO,
GIVEN BY KINGS WHO
WANTED TO WIN HER HAND!
THERE'S DANGER IN THE TANGO BAND!
WHEN SHE PLAYS UPON HER SOFT GUITAR,
SHE'D MAKE MILLIONS AS A MOVIE STAR.
SUCH A TEMPTATION, SUCH A SENSATION,
YOU DON'T KNOW WHERE YOU ARE.

THERE'S DANGER IN HER SOFT GUITAR.
SURELY SHE'S PERFECTION,
THAT BROWN COMPLEXION,
THAT JET-BLACK HAIR.
SHE WILL SMILE SO SWEETLY,
YOU'RE LOST COMPLETELY,
BEWARE! FOR
THERE'S A WOMAN IN THE TANGO BAND,
SHE'S THE TERROR OF THE TANGO BAND.
O SO ROMANTIC,
SHE'LL DRIVE YOU FRANTIC,
SO NOW YOU UNDERSTAND.
THERE'S DANGER IN THE TANGO BAND.

(Light laughter and applause are heard. An orchestral reprise begins and mixed chatter is heard.)

POIROT. Luigi! Luigi!

WAITER. Monsieur called?

POIROT. Mon vieux, I need some information.

WAITER. Always at your service, monsieur.

POIROT. I desire to know how many of these people at this table here have used the telephone tonight?

WAITER. I can tell you, monsieur. The young lady, the one in white, she telephoned at once when she got here. Then she went to leave her cloak, and while she was doing that, the other young lady came out of the cloakroom and went into the telephone box.

POIROT. So the señora did telephone! Was that *before* she came into the restaurant?

WAITER. Yes, monsieur.

POIROT. All this, Luigi, gives me furiously to think!

WAITER. Indeed, monsieur?

POIROT. Yes, I think, Luigi, that tonight of all nights, I must have my wits about me! Something is going to happen, Luigi, and I am not at all sure what it is.

WAITER. Anything I can do, monsieur?

POIROT. Thank you, Luigi. Leave me for a moment. Here is Mr. Carter coming back!

WAITER. Very good, monsieur!

(There is a slight pause.)

POIROT. Hélas! We are still deserted, Mr. Carter.

CARTER. Oh – er – quite.

POIROT. You know Mr. Barton Russell well?

CARTER. Yes, known him quite a good while.

POIROT. His sister-in-law, little Miss Weatherby, is very charming.

CARTER. Yes, pretty girl.

POIROT. You know her well, too?

CARTER. Quite.

POIROT. Oh quite, quite.

(Light applause is heard as the number ends. Mixed chatter is heard as guests return from the dance floor.)

RUSSELL. I hope we haven't left you too long, Monsieur Poirot?

POIROT. But no. I find much entertainment here.

RUSSELL. Ah, good. I'm glad of that. Come along, Lola. I want everyone here. I guess I've a little speech to make. Sit down, Pauline – you, too, Tony. That's right. Say, waiter, where's that bottle of champagne?

WAITER. Here sir, at once, sir.

RUSSELL. See here, folks, I'm going to ask you to drink a toast. To tell you the truth, there's an idea back of this little party tonight. As you know, I'd ordered a table for six. There were only five of us. That gave us an empty place. Then, by a very strange coincidence, Monsieur Hercule Poirot happened to pass by and I asked him to join our party. You don't know yet what an apt coincidence that was. You see that empty seat tonight represents a lady – the lady in whose memory this party is being given. This party, ladies and gentlemen, is being held in memory of my dear wife – Iris – who died exactly four years ago on this very date.

(There is a slight gasp from the guests.)

I'll ask you to drink to her memory. Iris!

POIROT. Iris?

OMNES. Iris – Iris... The flowers, don't you see? Yellow irises – etc., etc.

RUSSELL. It may seem odd to you all that I should celebrate the anniversary of a death in this way – by a supper party in a fashionable restaurant. But I have a reason, yes, I have a reason. For Monsieur Poirot's benefit, I'll explain.

PAULINE. But Barton –

RUSSELL. Please Pauline! Four years ago tonight, Monsieur Poirot, there was a supper party held at a club not unlike this in New York. At it were my wife and myself, Mr. Stephen Carter, who was attached to the embassy in Washington, Mr. Anthony Chappell, who had been a guest in our house for some weeks, and Señora Valdez, who was at that time enchanting New York City with her dancing. And, of course, my sister-in-law had unexpectedly come to stay. You remember, Pauline?

PAULINE. The weather had stopped me sailing home. I remember, yes.

RUSSELL. Monsieur Poirot, on that night a tragedy happened. There was a roll of drums and the cabaret started. The lights went down – all but a spot light in the middle of the floor. When the lights went up again, my wife was seen to have fallen forward on the table. She was dead – stone dead. There was potassium cyanide found in the dregs of her wine glass, and the remains of the packet were discovered in her handbag.

POIROT. She had committed suicide?

RUSSELL. That was the accepted verdict. It broke me, Monsieur Poirot. There was, perhaps, a possible reason for such an action – the police thought so. I accepted their decision.

(He beats his fist on table.)

But I was not satisfied. No, for four years I've been thinking and brooding and I'm not satisfied! I don't believe Iris killed herself. I believe, Monsieur Poirot, that she was murdered by one of those people at the table.

CHAPPELL. Look here, sir –

RUSSELL. Be quiet, Tony, I haven't finished. One of them did it, I'm sure of that now. Someone who, under cover of the darkness, slipped the half emptied packet of cyanide into her handbag. I think I know which of them it was. I mean to know the truth –

VALDEZ. You are mad – crazy – who would have harmed her? No, you are mad. Me, I will not stay –

POIROT. Gently, mademoiselle, gently.

> *(A roll of drums and cymbals are heard.* **RUSSELL** *speaks over the* **COMPERE** *who is heard in the background.)*

RUSSELL. The cabaret. Afterwards we will go on with this. Stay where you are, all of you. I've got to go and speak to the dance band leader. Little arrangement I've made with him.

COMPERE. Ladies and gentlemen. We now come to this evening's cabaret, in which we present first the celebrated torch singer, Inga Anderson in a number which she has brought with her from New York, where she sang it with great success. Here she is, ladies and gentlemen – Inga Anderson direct from New York – to sing you "Interrupted Rhythm!"

CARTER. Extraordinary business – man's mad.

VALDEZ. He is crazy, yes.

CHAPPELL. For two pins I'd clear out. I think we all ought to!

PAULINE. No!

> *(**PAULINE** speaks to herself.)*

Oh dear – oh dear –

POIROT. What is it, mademoiselle?

PAULINE. *(Whispers.)* It's horrible! It's just like it was that night.

EVERYONE. Shh! Shh!

POIROT. A little word in your ear. All will be well.

> *(Instrumental of "Interrupted Rhythm" begins to play.)*

VALDEZ. My God, listen!

POIROT. What is it, señora?

VALDEZ. It's the same tune – the same song that they played that night in New York. Barton Russell must have fixed it. I do not like this.

POIROT. Courage – courage.

["INTERRUPTED RHYTHM"]

IN THIS CIVILISATION, FULL OF MAD SYNCOPATION,
I GROW SICK OF THE DIN WE'RE MAKIN'.
THERE'S NO PLACE YOU CAN FLY TO,
IT'S NO GOOD IF YOU TRY TO,
EVERY NERVE IN YOUR BODY
IS SHAKIN' – BREAKIN',
WHETHER YOU'RE SLEEPIN' OR WAKIN'.

ALL ALONG THE MIDNIGHT HIGHWAY,
UNDERNEATH THE TRAFFIC'S ROAR,
THO' YOU MAY FEAR IT,
YOU'RE CERTAIN TO HEAR IT
INTERRUPTED RHYTHM DRUMMIN' LIKE WAR.
EVEN IN THE DARKENED BEDROOM,
WHERE IT'S NEVER BEEN BEFORE.
DRONIN' AND DRUMMIN', YOU'LL SOON HEAR IT COMIN'
INTERRUPTED RHYTHM IS AT THE DOOR.
WHILE I'M SINUOUSLY SWAYING, THROUGH THE LIMELIGHT,
GAILY DRESSED,
THERE'S A HEART IN ME IS PRAYING FOR THE SHANTY,
OUT WEST, WHERE THERE IS REST.
MILLIONS OF CRAZY PEOPLE JOGGIN' ON THE JAZZ BAND FLOOR.
JUST AS I'M SPEAKIN' ARE EVERYWHERE SHRIEKIN',
INTERRUPTED RHYTHM, GIVE US SOME MORE!

(A burst of applause is heard, as the song ends.)

WAITER. Champagne, miss? Champagne, sir?

CHAPPELL. She's great, that girl! Lord, what a voice!

VALDEZ. *(Screaming.)* Look! Look!

CHAPPELL. Pauline! Darling!

VALDEZ. She's dead! Just like Iris – like Iris in New York!

POIROT. Quickly there. Draw the curtain, nobody must see!

RUSSELL. But it's impossible, she can't be dead!

POIROT. Yes, she is dead – la pauvre petite. And I, sitting by her! Ah! But this time the murderer shall not escape!

RUSSELL. Just like Iris! She saw something – Pauline saw something that night only she wasn't sure – she told me she wasn't sure! We must get the police! Oh God, my poor Pauline!

POIROT. No, no, we can do without the police! Where is her glass? Yes, I can smell the cyanide. A smell of bitter almonds. The same method, the same poison. Let us look in her handbag.

RUSSELL. You don't believe this is suicide, too? Not on your life.

POIROT. Wait. No, there is nothing here. The lights went up, you see, too quickly – the murderer had not time. Therefore, the poison is still on him.

CARTER. Or her.

VALDEZ. What do you mean – what do you say? That I kill her! It is not true – not true! Why should I do such a thing!

POIROT. Really, Mr. Carter!

CARTER. You had rather a fancy for Barton Russell yourself in New York. That's the gossip I heard. Argentine beauties are notoriously jealous.

VALDEZ. That is a pack of lies! And I do not come from the Argentine. I come from Peru. Ah, I spit upon you – I –

(She lapses into Spanish in her anger.)

POIROT. I demand silence. It is for me to speak.

RUSSELL. Everyone must be searched.

POIROT. *(Calmly.)* Non, non, it is not necessary.

RUSSELL. What d'you mean, not necessary?

POIROT. I, Hercule Poirot, know. I see with the eyes of the mind. And I will speak! Monsieur Carter, will you show us the packet in your breast pocket?

CARTER. There's nothing in my pocket. What the hell –

POIROT. Tony, my good friend, if you will be so obliging.

CARTER. Damn you – take your hands away!

CHAPPELL. There you are, Poirot. Just as you said – a packet!

CARTER. It's a damned lie!

POIROT. Cyanide of potassium. The case is complete.

RUSSELL. Carter! I always thought so. Iris was in love with you. She wanted to go away with you. You didn't want a scandal for the sake of your precious career, so you poisoned her. You'll hang for this, you dirty dog.

POIROT. Silence! This is not finished yet. I, Hercule Poirot, have something to say. My friend here, Tony Chappell, he says to me when I arrive, that I have come in search of crime. That, it is partly true. There was crime in my mind – but it was to prevent a crime that I came. And I have prevented it. The murderer, he planned well – but Hercule Poirot he was one move ahead. He had to think fast, and to whisper quickly in mademoiselle's ear when the lights went down. She is very quick and clever, Mademoiselle Pauline, she played her part well. Mademoiselle, will you be so kind as to show us that you are not dead after all?

(**PAULINE** *laughs shakily.*)

PAULINE. Resurrection of Pauline.

(*Everybody gasps.*)

CHAPPELL. Pauline – darling!

PAULINE. Tony!

CHAPPELL. My sweet!

PAULINE. Angel!

RUSSELL. I – I don't understand...

POIROT. I will help you to understand, Mr. Barton Russell. Your plan has miscarried.

RUSSELL. My plan?

POIROT. Yes, your plan. Who was the only man who had an alibi during the darkness? The man who left the table. You, Mr. Barton Russell. But you returned to it under cover of the darkness, circling round it, with a champagne bottle, filling up glasses, putting cyanide in Pauline's glass and dropping the half empty packet in Carter's pocket as you bent over him to remove a glass. Oh yes, it is easy to play the part of a waiter in darkness when the attention of everyone is elsewhere. That was the real reason for your party tonight. The safest place to commit a murder is in the middle of a crowd.

RUSSELL. What the – why the hell should I want to kill Pauline?

POIROT. It might be, perhaps, a question of money. Your wife left you guardian to her sister. You mentioned that fact tonight. Pauline is twenty. At twenty-one, or on her marriage, you would have to render an account of your stewardship. I suggest that you could not do that. You have speculated with it. I do not know, Mr. Barton Russell, whether you killed your wife in the same way, or whether her suicide suggested the idea of this crime to you, but I do know that tonight you have been guilty of attempted murder. It rests with Miss Pauline whether you are prosecuted for that.

PAULINE. No. He can get out of my sight and out of this country. I don't want another scandal.

POIROT. You had better go quickly, Mr. Barton Russell, and I advise you to be careful in future.

RUSSELL. To hell with you, you interfering little Belgian jackanapes.

POIROT. *(Threateningly.)* Goodbye, Mr. Russell.

RUSSELL. Bah!

(There is a pause.)

POIROT. And that, my friends, is that!

PAULINE. Monsieur Poirot, you've been wonderful.

POIROT. You, mademoiselle, you have been the marvellous one. To pour away the champagne, to act the dead body so prettily.

PAULINE. Ugh! You give me the creeps.

POIROT. It was you who telephoned me, was it not?

PAULINE. Yes.

POIROT. Why?

PAULINE. I don't know. I was worried and frightened, without knowing quite why I was frightened. Barton told me he was having this party to commemorate Iris' death. I realised he had some scheme on, but he wouldn't tell me what it was. He looked so – so queer and so excited that I felt something terrible might happen. Only, of course, I never dreamt that he meant to – to get rid of me.

POIROT. And so, mademoiselle?

PAULINE. I'd heard Tony talking about you. I thought if I could only get you here perhaps it would stop anything happening. I thought that being a – a foreigner, if I rang up and pretended to be in danger and – and made it sound mysterious –

POIROT. You thought the melodrama, it would attract me? That is what puzzled me – the message itself – definitely it was what you call "bogus." It did not ring true. But the fear in the voice – that was real. Then I came and you denied, very categorically, having sent me a message.

PAULINE. I had to. Besides, I didn't want you to know it was me.

POIROT. Ah. I was fairly sure of that! Not at first. But I soon realised that the only two people who could know about the yellow irises on the table were you or Mr. Barton Russell.

PAULINE. Yes, I heard him ordering them to be put on the table. That, and his ordering a table for six, when I knew only five were coming, made me suspect.

POIROT. What did you suspect, mademoiselle?

PAULINE. I was afraid of something happening to – Mr. Carter.

POIROT. Mr. Carter – so?

CARTER. Er – hm – I have to – er – thank you, Monsieur Poirot. I owe you a great deal. You'll excuse me, I'm sure, if I leave you. Tonight's happenings have been – rather upsetting. Goodnight. Goodnight.

(There is a pause.)

PAULINE. *(Violently.)* I hate him. I've always thought it was because of him that Iris killed herself. Or perhaps, Barton killed her. Oh it's all so hateful!

POIROT. Forget, mademoiselle.

(The orchestra starts a slow foxtrot.)

Forget. Let the past go. Think only of the present.

PAULINE. Yes – you're right.

POIROT. Señora Valdez, as the evening advances I become more brave. If you would dance with me now –

VALDEZ. Oh yes, indeed. You are – you are the cat's whiskers, Monsieur Poirot. I insist on dancing with you. After tonight's happening I need the protection of such a man as you!

POIROT. You are too kind, señora. To dance with Señora Lola Valdez is indeed an honour.

VALDEZ. *(Laughing.)* Oh, Monsieur Poirot, you flatterer. Ha! Ha! Ha!

CHAPPELL. Pauline – Pauline.

PAULINE. Yes, Tony?

CHAPPELL. Darling.

PAULINE. Oh, Tony, I've been such a nasty, spiteful, spit-firing little cat to you all day. Can you ever forgive me?

CHAPPELL. Angel! This is our tune again. Let's dance.

PAULINE. Of course, my sweet.

(The restaurant chatter fades with a vocal refrain of "You Live In My Heart.")

["YOU LIVE IN MY HEART"]

SINGER.
>YOU LIVE IN MY HEART,
>AND YOU'RE A PART OF ALL THE LOVELINESS I SEE.

TOGETHER.
>YOU LIVE IN MY DREAMS,
>EVEN THE SCHEMES
>I MAKE ARE FASHIONED FOR YOU ONLY.
>YOU LIVE IN MY HEART,
>NO MATTER HOW THE WAVES OF OCEAN ROLL BETWEEN.

SINGER.
>RIGHT, RIGHT FROM THE START,
>I'VE ALWAYS HELD YOU CLOSE
>FOR YOU LIVE IN MY HEART.

TOGETHER.
>YOU EVER LIVE IN MY HEART.

End of Play

THE AGATHA CHRISTIE COLLECTION

Agatha Christie is regarded as the most successful female playwright of all time. Her illustrious dramatic career spans forty-two years, countless acclaimed original plays, several renowned novels adapted for stage, and numerous collections of thrilling one-act plays. Testament to Christie's longevity, these plays continue to engage great artists and enthral audiences today.

Since the première of her first play in 1930 the world of theatre has changed immeasurably, and so has the way plays are published and performed. Embarking upon a two-year project, Agatha Christie Limited sought to re-open Christie's distinguished body of dramatic work, looking to both original manuscripts and the most recent publications to create a "remastered" edition of each play. Each new text would contain only the words of Agatha Christie (or adaptors she personally worked with) and all extraneous materials that might come between the interpreter and the playwright would be removed, ultimately bringing the flavor and content of the texts closer to what the author would have delivered to the rehearsal room. Each new edition would then be specifically tailored to the needs and requirements of the professional twenty-first century artist.

The result is The Collection.

Whether in a classic revival or new approach, The Collection has been purposely assembled for the contemporary theatre professional. The choice and combination of plays offers something for all tastes and kinds of performance with the skill, imagination and genius of Agatha Christie's work now waiting to be explored anew in theatre.

For more information on The Collection, please visit
agathachristielimited.com/licensing/stage/browse-by-play

www.ingramcontent.com/pod-product-compliance
Ingram Content Group UK Ltd.
Pitfield, Milton Keynes, MK11 3LW, UK
UKHW021848210426
5322IPUK00022B/536